A Dress Walked By With a Woman Inside

A Dress Walked By With a Woman Inside

New & Selected Poetry & Prose

MICHAEL G. HICKEY

NCP
Northchester Press
northchesterpress.com

Published in the United States by Northchester Press

The Cataloging-in-Publication Data is on file with
the Library of Congress

ISBN: 978-1-47746-605-6

NorthchesterPress.com

Design: SONYA UNREIN
Cover art: MICHAEL WARLUM

Printed in the United States of America

"Poetic Justice" *Abbey*; "Linda's Home Improvement Loan" & "Don't Read This Poem" *Atlanta Review*; "Dove" *Atom Mind*; "Love Poem" *Bellowing Ark*; "Unsolicited Material" *Black Cross*; "The Boy in Third Grade" winner of the Candlelight Poetry Award, *Candlelight Poetry Journal*; "Tuesday" *Crab Creek Review*; "The Comeback" *CrazyQuilt*; "Fifth Grade Show & Tell," "Two ears, One mouth," "Prison Poetry," "I Should Tell You Right Now," "Equilibrium" *Crosscurrents*; "Direction of the Spiral" *Curriculum Vitae Literary Supplement*; "The House I Grew Up In" *Gazoobi Press*; "Tiger Tamer" *Permafrost*; "Why I Want to Give You My Hat" *PongoTeenWriting.org*; "Twenty Years Ago," "Poetry Graveyard" *Spindrift*; "My Life as a Woman from Cleveland" *Seattle Review;* Prepare for Take-off, *Cedars Literary Journal.*

For my raison d'etre Ramona, Nathan, and T.J.

Thanks to Stephanie Hallgren, Richard Shelton, Nelson Bentley, Heather McHugh, and Michael Ryan. Thanks also to Richard Gold and Pongo Teen Poetry. Finally, thanks to teachers and students past, present, future and to the family and friends who sustain me.

Contents

The Cage Door

—for Stephanie Hallgren, 5/21/11

Know this:
for every phony from *Catcher in the Rye*
revered by applauding saguaros, player pianos,
& accolades standing in line,
there is an antidote in a long white dress with strawberry hair.

I know ballyhoo & people famous with a small "f"
whose peanut is more like a shell
or the two rodent parts per million
allowed in canned chili. I'm ashamed to admit
I sometimes beg them to tattoo my scars

with their approval. But it is a lucky sleep indeed
to dream of you, or at least the idea of you:
the leap second to correct atomic clocks,
blue mountains in love,
the whisper of hands praying in supplication.

On the day the world is scheduled to end,
the only revelation I see is a river running with hope.
Because haven't you heard?
The eye of the storm is myopic.
The door of my cage has been lifted.

The Boy in Third Grade

1.

Telephone rings in the middle
of my chicken noodle soup.

I'm not selling anything, the man says.
Would you mind answering a few survey questions?
It'll only take five minutes.

Okay.

What do you do for a living?

Poet.

The anonymous interviewer chuckles.
Seriously sir, what is your occupation?

2.

Later, I ponder the origin of this pursuit
that strokes the mirth of inquisitive strangers
& I keep going back to the boy in third grade.
Greg with the green shirt,
who made Mrs. Denzer blush.
We were all in love with her,
staying after school to clean erasers
lower shades, pilfer whiffs of her perfume.

She taught us about poems,
why she liked them, why we should, too.
Her eyes green as Greg's shirt.
At the end of class everyone wrote one.

Greg read his & her cheeks transformed
into American Beauty roses,
her eyes filled with wet adrenaline.
The fat smile on Greg's face, my envy like a hemorrhage
in the sweet moist air. She said he had written
the most beautiful poem she ever read
& I still remember the first line:

A dress walked by with a woman inside.

Dear Mikey

You are five years old today, and the year is 1961. I am writing you from 2005, 44 years later, and I have a lot to say. Today mom and dad told you that you were adopted. They explained it to you very well. They said that mommy and daddy wanted you, and that a woman who had you in her tummy and couldn't take care of you decided to give you to mommy and daddy. This was the greatest day in their lives.

It all seemed right, like no one was trying to trick you. But then you asked, "Mom, where's my real mom?" This broke her heart, and she cried in her room all day and wouldn't come out. She wouldn't let daddy in either. He slept on the couch that night. You didn't know why she was crying, so now I'm going to explain it to you.

Mommy and daddy tried to have a baby for seven years. One of mom's favorite stories was when she went to a state fair and visited a fortune teller. She was Catholic and didn't really believe in fortune tellers, but she went anyway just for fun. The strangely dressed woman read mom's palm and told her in the future she would have seven children. Mom laughed as her and dad hadn't had any luck in having even one. And as it turned out, the fortune teller was wrong. Mom didn't have seven kids. She had eleven!

After they adopted you, mom got pregnant right away. There was some question then as to whether or not they were still going to adopt you since they were going to have their own, but mom told the lawyers, "That's my baby." So the lawyers made sure you were adopted. Shortly thereafter, mom had twins named Timmy and Jimmy. But unfortunately, they died at the age of one and two weeks. Then mom and dad had four more boys and four more girls. They all lived and became your brothers and sisters, and here's a little secret for you: I think you were always mom's favorite. She let you stay up later than anyone else and often made your favorite dinner, spaghetti, which you pronounced, "sketti." You would say hello to anyone and everyone, and whenever mom or dad asked you to say a word, you'd always give it a try. You were also very proud of all your various potty training accomplishments in the bathroom. One time you stuffed wads of toilet paper in your pants just in case you "had an accident."

As time went on, you wondered more and more about your "real" mom. Who was she? What did she look like? Why did she give you away? Where was she now? And when your adopted mom died of cancer in 1978, you started wondering about your biological mother even more. You were hurt and confused. I understand that.

But now, Mikey, I'm writing you to define the word "real." Your real mom was your adopted mom. She did everything for you: fed you, bathed you, stayed in your room when you had German measles and couldn't hear for two days. Most of all, she loved you. She loved you more than life itself. If she were here today, she'd tell you that and you'd know you don't have to wonder about your real mom anymore. The woman who gave you birth is an important person. She made a brave decision and gave you the gift of life. But your real mom was named Elaine. If there's a God in heaven and I believe there is, then she's up there waiting for you, your brothers and sisters, and your dad. Some day everything will be explained. Some day all will be revealed. But you should also know that some day you will have a child of your own, and you'll love that baby as much as Elaine loved you. Imagine that. In a world full of rain, one drop will belong to you. That is something wonderful to remember. So work hard in school, have fun in life, and remember that love interlocks the universe. Nothing can ever change that. *Real* is a word. *Real* is a just a word. What is real is what you know in your heart is real.

Fifth Grade Show & Tell

Roberta Butz's dad owns a slaughterhouse
where mother buys sides of beef at a discount.
I really like Bobbie Butz, you know, for a girl,
& on show-and-tell day
she proudly displays a cow's eye
floating in a jar of formaldehyde.

Eileen Olrich, the smartest girl in school,
straight-A student with more stars
on her progress chart than the Milky Way.
She makes eye contact with the cow's eye.
Her face immediately blanches like a bleached sock
the color drains from scalp to chin
& slowly she starts to swirl
        like an old-time
record player
        scratching out a 45

until she trembles, faints, & falls on the floor
imploding like an old building on the evening news.
Sister Mary Frances rushes to her aid
& all I can think is oh how I love thee,
fifth grade, fifth grade.

Love Poem

1.

Twinkle, Twinkle,
little star, You're my
girl friend, You are! You are!

Roses are red,
Violets are blue,
I hope you like me,
'cause I like you!

2.

the first poem I ever wrote
was the worst poem I ever wrote
except to her, Ellen Curell
my second grade girlfriend

eyes blue as Planet Earth
viewed by astronauts in space
bangs, dimples, pleated skirt & knee socks
she showed me her appendectomy scar at twilight
behind the baseball diamond at St, Augustine's

my composition for her
was re-copied in gold ink by Jim
my next-door neighbor
an eighth grader with perfect cursive
that flowed like calligraphy on fire
& the next day
when Sister Mary Peter turned her back in class

I slipped the poem to Ellen
whose smile spread like ocean waves in slow motion

but later that month her dad got transferred
Ellen's family moved to Mt. Vernon
sixty miles away
which might as well have been Hong Kong
& all that week I cried myself to sleep
didn't eat, didn't even watch TV

3.

fifteen years later, home from college
on summer break at the county fair
between the cotton candy & Tilt-A-Whirl
a friend leads me to the parking lot
someone I have to see
& there she is – Ellen Curell
leaning against a pickup truck
still those blueplanet eyes

hugs, small talk, remember second grade?
just before we leave forever again
she says, "Wait" & from the darkest African regions of her wallet
she pulls out the poem, the poem in gold ink
paper tattered, yellow as a harvest moon
& it occurs to me in the parking lot
alive with rainbow snow cones & blue ribbon chrysanthemums
I may have peaked as a poet with the first poem I ever wrote
an astronaut on a mission
planting flags & stomping around
on the chalkdust of a twinkling little star

To the Girl in Sophomore Biology

I can't stop staring at you, sitting in that shaft of sunshine
by the windows in the sixth row

and it doesn't help knowing your cells are extinguishing
like thousands of tiny campfires on the beach

despite the fact they are constantly replacing themselves.
In fact, according to Professor Throckmorton,

the entire topography of your skin
will regenerate itself in 28 days.

Just think, a month ago
your entire shell was a completely different you.

And incredibly you're recreating yourself
without even trying!

I find it even more amazing that somehow
I manage to love each new you a little more than the last.

Identifying the Enemy, 1974

determined to serve, protect & save my Catholic high school
from the scourge of illegal drugs
the local police arrive to modest fanfare
on a Friday morning in February
without uniforms or riot gear
no billyclubs twirling like batons in a holiday parade
no tear gas canisters or handcuffs
not even a lousy service revolver strapped to a bulletproof vest
the war on drugs is a war without weapons
at least it is in my Catholic high school
Our Lady of Great Scrutiny

wide-eyed teenagers gather as if at a surgical procedure
squinting at the assorted tools of the drug trade:
bongs, water pipes, rolling papers, rolling machines
roach clips, super chargers, fake joints & more paraphernalia
the detectives take turns explaining each exhibit's purpose
if we are, say, at a party, the taller detective explains
& see any of these items we should:

calmly but quickly leave the premises
summon the authorities, run in front of a car
set something on fire—but get the heck out of there!

the other detective suggests we watch
Reefer Madness & discuss it with our parents

by afternoon homeroom, 47 of 50 exhibits
missing or otherwise unaccounted for
rumors, threats & innuendoes
begin to spin devil dervishes through the dusty halls
suspensions & expulsions are guaranteed

resounding verbal indictments reverberate off the walls
graduation postponed, cancelled, criminal charges loom…

our entire school learned a valuable lesson that day
not about drugs, but that our principal, Father Ryan
could make his face turn the same color
as a tomato in my mother's garden
& his vocabulary could send a man of the cloth straight to hell

Love Letters from Goliath's Ex-Girlfriend

The stars in Nishran's eyes are always on the verge of combustion. Her eyebrows live in separate worlds yet long for one another. Her lips speak the body language of the moon, and the neck that leads to her heart is the same neck that remembers what every other neck has forgotten ages ago. She is a Philistine who loves Hebrews. She is a fallen star that will not stop shining.

Goliath herds sheep and at nightfall whispers to bleating lambs abandoned by their mothers. He loves Nishy. He has always loved Nishy. But what with tending his flock for weeks at a time, he and Nishy barely keep company. One night at a harvest feast, she is in the embrace of Omni, a warrior known for his fearlessness in battle. Goliath can't stop staring at them. When he can bear it no longer, he draws his sword and threatens to kill the philanderer. Nishy throws herself at Goliath's feet. She shows him the love letters she has scribed daily for a fortnight proclaiming her fidelity, her devotion, letters she keeps in a leather pouch next to her heart. In these letters, she praises Omni's eyes, worships his war wounds, and swoons over the musk of his scent after battle. "He's the only man I've ever loved. If you have to kill someone," she exclaims, "kill me for I am nothing without Omni!" She points at her belly. "Already I carry the fruit of his loins in my womb." Deep inside Goliath, a bright light darkens into an elongated shadow. A contorted silhouette.

He commences to drinking gourds of wine from morning to night and fighting Philistines he once called friends. He wants men to fear him not because of his size—four cubits and a span—but because he doesn't have the heart to hate Nishy so he hates himself instead. Contempt is the air he breathes even in his dreams.

This is what love can do when it turns. One day you've got a good job and you're in love. The sunset splashes the horizon with its palette of purples and pinks and each of your bones feels as lucky as a wishbone. Then you blink your eye for an instant and the next thing you know you're felled by a midget with a couple river rocks and a mandate from on High. This is the kind of love that makes wild dogs howl at the moon. This is the kind of love in which being beheaded by your own sword is an act of compassion, a giant favor.

Dove

Aquamarine mohawk, nose ring, dragon tattoo
on upper arm. Her name is Elizabeth Shortley, but
she prefers to be called *Dove*.
"I hope we're not gonna waste the whole semester
talking about a bunch of old farts
who've been dead a hundred years," she says.

The first exercise is to write at the speed of sound
for five minutes. Fill up as much of the page as possible.
If you need a jump start, use any color of the rainbow
& as if by design, I point out the window
to a rainbow on the horizon appearing like a prop.
There is no better sound than the collective silence
of twenty people writing as fast as they can.

When time expires, Dove volunteers to read.
Her title, "My Green Vulva"
but someone coughs & I hear, "My Green Volvo."
By the third stanza it becomes abundantly clear
the poem has no relation to the world's safest automobile.
I praise Dove for the inventiveness & innovation in her writing.
The class seems to sense the trepidation in my voice.

The next week I encourage students
to play God & write an obituary
for the person of their choice.
Combat boots marching to the front of the room,
Dove recites her newest offering
about a poetry writing instructor
gunned down in an underground parking garage.

Elizabeth Shortley, alias Dove, successfully completes
"Introduction to Poetry Writing." I see her name
on next semester's list for "Intermediate Poetry Writing."
I should warn the teacher, Todd, an arrogant son of a bitch
who claims to be related to Walt Whitman
but decide instead to wait until the second week
& give Dove a crack at Todd's first assignment:
Memorize & Deconstruct Lord Byron.

How to Avoid Spills

In the kitchen,
my mother sings hymns
arias
& assorted show tunes
when she carries
        the ice cube tray
                        full of water
                                from the sink to the freezer.

She has a theory that singing prevents spills.

Outside the kitchen window
three seagulls
fight a forty mile-an-hour headwind
swooping and diving over rooftops and treetops
listening for any scrap of my mother's voice.

How to Make Women Want You

rims.
26-inch
with
stroller
red
a
in
baby
adorable
an
pushing
hill
steep
a
up

Walk

How to Spark Your Monkey

"Ms. Nguyen," I address a shy Vietnamese girl with silk black hair in the first row. "Have you selected a topic for your process essay?"

"Yes teacher," she whispers. "How to Spark Your Monkey."

"How to Spark Your Monkey?"

The advanced students in back giggle. One finally one explains, "She's not saying *How to Spark Your Monkey*, she saying *How to Save Your Money.*"

The entire class cackles, even Ms. Nguyen. But take away the sexual innuendo. What if someone really did own a bored gorilla, an apathetic ape. I implore Ms. Nguyen to explore that possibility. An essay on How to Spark Your Monkey will be infinitely more engaging and compelling than another rehash about carpooling and clipping coupons.

First, get primal with your primate. Swim the breaststroke deep into the wet pools of his eyes. Listen to the percussion of his heart. What does the music suggest to you about empathy, sympathy, consolation? Be proud to pound your chest. Carry his pain as if it is your own child because in the big scheme of things goddammit it is your own child and your own pain and you should eat a banana or two and swing on a vine. Understand that somewhere out there, in a state of utter hopelessness and lethargy, a dispassionate chimp is lost asunder. Instruct your readers to cherish this beast every minute of every day because life could end any instant, even before they finish reading your essay.

On Monday Ms. Nguyen submits her new essay, "How to Choose Your College Major."

Another Reason to Hate Rich People

I.

Red hair, barbed wire & snake tattoos, chains, black leather jacket & a beat-up Harley parked illegally. He staggers into Animal Control where every year we *transition* 16,000 lost dogs & cats into 16,000 cans of dog & cat food. He's holding a dead pit bull in his arms.

I was late for work. The only morning I didn't pet him. Halfway down the road, I came back to get my wallet and there he was, dead, hanging over the fence. He just wanted to say goodbye before I left for work . . . I loved that dog. I loved that dog more than I loved my own life. He deposits Buster on the floor in an old quilt, a sacrificial offering to an angry God, and walks out the front door without looking back.

II.

Just before closing, a middle-aged couple wheels up in a convertible white Jag. She places a pink cat carrier on the counter with the word AL-CAT-TRAZ on top. Inside squirms a Siamese, white with tan markings, determined to make eye contact. The woman is dripping in bling and wearing a short black cocktail dress. *We've changed the décor of our winter condo from Oriental to Early American. We no longer wish to keep this animal.* As she says this, her man checks his watch and uses a toothpick to pluck something from between his teeth.

Why I Want to Give You My Hat

I'll never forget that day after poetry class
when the ghost inside your shadow confided
your grandmother had died
& your boyfriend had moved to Oklahoma
to be with his ailing mother.
What will you do without him?
I'll never forget the soft chocolate brown of your eyes
when you asked if I thought you were still a virgin
even though, technically,
your father stole that from you every night for a month.
I asked if your boyfriend knew—maybe you should tell him
'cause wouldn't you want to know?
And whether or not your father is really your stepfather
I don't know
but the more you hate him,
the more you let him keep your power,
& maybe you should forgive him,
not because he deserves it,
but because you do.

I know you were wondering why you were telling me all this
more or less a stranger with nothing more than a red pen
so now I'm going to explain it to you.
Poetry opens these viaducts & tear ducts & trap doors.
It's more dependable than people making promises.
It changes like the weather but like the weather,
it never goes away.

The world is in constant need of love & consolation.
We can't change the way we think to change the way we live,
we have to change the way we live to change the way we think.

I want to give you my hat to protect the dreams in your head
from all the people who have recklessly wasted their own
& will only feel better when they can kill yours.
I want to give you a sacrosanct cloud to float on.
I want to give you relief from the gathering storm.

That day after poetry class I went to a faculty meeting
& I don't have the vaguest idea what any of them said
because I couldn't stop thinking
about why the world is so fucked up sometimes,
& I wish I didn't have to write this poem but I do,
to save my own life even if I can't help to save yours.

Ten Years

you are a dragon
you are a green dragon with a long tail
you are a three-year-old green dragon
with a long green tail and big green spikes on Halloween
you walk up to the first house, but do not knock on the door
or shout *trick-or-treat* but instead step right inside
the homeowner screams—*someone is breaking & entering*!
it is a three-year-old green dragon roaming her living room
this is worth an extra handful of candy corn

ten years later
you're reppin' the hood, bangin' on Hofstra Boulevard
slangin' ice in the streets, giving oral sex
to a fat 40-year-old in a blue shirt
with crazy eyes and when you're finished
he holds a .357 magnum
to the soft blonde hair at your left temple
he wants his $60 back
his voice sounds like a parrot's
after he gets his money
he makes you walk backwards, away from the car
you think *this is it, this is where it all ends*
but he doesn't shoot you after all
he just didn't want you to see his license plate

you go home & step inside the green door without knocking
tell your mother that an hour ago
a john held a gun to your head
she does not scream or give you candy
she says she thought you weren't doing that anymore
but her eyes never leave the TV

she is watching something too important to miss
her favorite movie from a decade ago
she is engrossed in the characters, perplexed by the plot
maybe it will all end differently this time
not like the last time or the time before that
& she will not notice as you leave the house
nor will she hear the screen door slam
or the wind rattle the thin armor of its fragile threshold

Spin Cycle

Tammy turns tricks on the street like her mother did
even though she knows it's wrong.

Luther's incarcerated for slangin' ice like his old man. His little
brother wants to be in juvie just like him someday.

Billy cuts his finger with a pocketknife. The wound is deep.
He expects blood but instead witnesses a steady stream of
bad news. This is the moment his father would have kicked
something and unleashed a series of invectives so toxic
the neighbors would bubble-wrap their DNA and rent a moving
van. Billy looks at his finger. What will he kick?

When Daisy crashes her bike at the bottom of the cemetery hill
where her mother is buried, the fender is dented and the rear
wheel spins at a slight angle. Will she muster the strength
to jam a stick in the spokes and stop the gears?

Will the planets continue to revolve around the sun even though
they know Pluto has been demoted?

And what will it take to sneak up on the apple and kick it from
the tree's elongated shadow as daylight continues to wane?

Living Inside Out

In a field I am the absence of field. This is always the case.
Wherever I am I am what's missing.
—"Keeping Things Whole" Mark Strand

juvenile detention, a dark matinee
in time my eyes will adjust to the muted light
to walking single file, hands behind my back
in time I will no longer miss the oppression of the sun
or the tyranny of July

when I examine the 116 cuts on my arms
I will remember each of their tiny tragedies:

#1—my father in my bed
#33—shooting dope in my foot
#47—mother MIA
#54—brother in my bed
#71—pimp's meth habit
#77—pimp's wild eyes
#83—brother, again
#99—pimp's fist
#116—some crazy fuck from Florida holding a gun to my head

someday I will step outside of this theater
& 116 diminutive shafts of light
will slant upward from my arms toward the sky
I will wonder then if I am destined
to return to the dark light of this matinee
whether or not I will finally be able to see
that which I have been unable to see before

Two Ears, One Mouth

the razor blade's tic-tic-tic as it chops the blow
the persistent wail of the siren
the frenzied footsteps racing around the duplex
the crinkle of paper under the bed
the flush of the toilet
the rhythmic inhaling and exhaling
the metallic click of the handcuffs
the mechanical recitation of Miranda rights
the slam of the squad car door
the metallic thunk of my cell door closing
the nervous tap of a plastic spoon in mess hall
the clip-clop of flip-flops shuffling in single file
the judge's verdict, her voice devoid of emotion
my mother's sniffling
the inconsistent percussion of my father's ailing heart
the engine of the van transferring me to Echo Glen
the guard's cackle and chuckle
at another guard's dirty joke
the desperate snoring of my new cellie
the groans, shouts, and cries
every night from every corner of cell block "C"
the cells of my DNA conspiring to escape
the sound of the voice in my head
which is not an auditory hallucination
repeating over and over with the beat of a metronome
you will only be as happy as you decide you want to be

The Light of Roscoe's Intentions

"We tend to see ourselves primarily in the light of our intentions, which are invisible to others. But we see others in the light of their actions, which are visible to us." —J.G. Bennett

Roscoe is being led out of Youth Detention, hands behind his back,
along with four months, two weeks,
and three days of good behavior
for assault with a deadly weapon, a class-three felony.
Roscoe has a bird of prey's face. He is gangly, 6'4", sixteen,
blond hair with hotrod red highlights and a blue tattoo
around his right wrist featuring a snake eating another snake.

One day Roscoe does a gram of coke, a bottle of Nyquil,
and goes to school. In retrospect, he realizes this was a mistake.
In the boys bathroom on the third floor of Mt. Hopewell High,
Steven Wellington has the temerity to step on Roscoe's toe.
This was Steven Wellington's mistake.
The deadly weapon was 312 pages of sophomore algebra,
the most use Roscoe ever got out of that damn book.
Steven Wellington would recover. He always did.

And it did not help that in literature class
when the instructor suggested
that most poems were about sex or death,
Roscoe replied, "You'd think there'd be
more poems about necrophilia."

What Roscoe sees in himself is this:
a teenager too smart for school,
too bored and impatient for the monotony of academe,
tired of taking orders from people who know less than he does.

He sees himself as a star that is creating its own lexicon,
climbing the horizon and glowing like a neon marble.

But what Roscoe's mother sees is not what Roscoe says
but what Roscoe does. And as she meets him on the free-
dom side of the electronic weapons scanner,
he is momentarily transformed into a little boy again.
Freckles. Dimples. Eyes that smile. A need to be held.
But soon – this was the pattern –
Roscoe would revert back to his old ways:
shooting dope, home invasion, vandalism.
He is slowly becoming her ex-husband:
angry, violent, detached. Living in a state that begins with an
"I."

One night many years from now,
Roscoe's mom will be driving and see her son
balanced
precariously on the seawall
in a driving thunderstorm. Lightning crackles over the bay,
over the whitecapped waves. Wind and torrents of rain
pummel him. The moon illuminates
the restless breakers and the insolent surf
as it sprays her only son.
Is he thinking of that last day in juvie?
Of Steven Wellington, who died in a fire that winter?
Is he thinking of his father doing five-to-ten in Walla Walla
for distribution of a controlled substance,
and the class-one felony of being a negligent father?

This drenched man
clearly courting death by drowning,
does not move nor wipe his brow.
He does not tip off his next move

nor reveal the apex of the arc
in the tragic trajectory of his intention.
Roscoe's mother will park the car and turn off the lights.
She has to see if it is really him or just someone
who looks like him from a distance in the rain
because her eyes aren't what they used to be.

Prison Poetry

right off I say *fuck* a few times
hope this will boost my credibility
one prisoner says he played baseball
for Washington State University
one can recite Plath chapter & verse
another will not share his name or make eye contact
but like the Indian in *Cuckoo's Nest*
at the end of class I realize he is neither deaf nor dumb
he hands me a page of profound, moving verse about slave ships
his pencil has a graphite flow of calligraphy
& despite my claustrophobia, it is a good day
the men thank me, appreciative
they look forward to the next class
I exchange the prison I.D. for my driver's license
a Correctional Officer says, "Today was visiting day
and you were their only visitor"
it is dark outside, I back the car out of the lot
there are strobe lights
the sharpshooter in the tower shouts through the bullhorn
"Do not proceed in reverse. Pull forward around the parking lot."
"OK," I scream, hands covering my eyes.
"Don't shoot. I'm only a poet!"
later I learn the prisoners made a wager
whether or not the poet will return next month
because no one ever does who doesn't have to

For The New Boss

oh queen of the whoops & sycamore trees
oh redolent splendor of haikus in a hurricane
when the sky gets the wind kicked out of it
& can't catch its breath
when giggles begin at the sight of geese
            honking gaggles in arrowhead formations
                    dipping their wings & singing your praises
                                accompanied by the harmonious congress
in your root cellar

all for you my love!

alley cats mark tailpipes with furry chins
fans on rooftops, lepers in treetops
helicopters, champagne
the easy listening sounds of cool jazz
& a body of white smoke from every chimney

each of us love you
in our own fabulous costume & mask
each of us part of the rally
even the player to be named later
who has blood-doped himself
head-over-heels
into this elusive sleight-of-hand

Outside

there is snow on snow
a dog barking plaintively at the newspaper carrier

I stare at the flicker of the flame
think of lovers who left my bed

who couldn't sleep in a place
so foreign, so benign

insomnia is a constant companion
it reminds me there is no substitute for pain

it is enough to make me question
the existence of a god

the existence of you
and in my hand I hold an ancient Roman coin

my father gave me before he died
I turn it over and over as I watch the candle's battle

against time
I consider the hands that held it before me

flip it in the air
ascend, descend – heads, tails

trying to convince myself the choice is mine, not yours

Concerning Miss Helen Crump: The Shelf Life of Perfection

—for Aneta C.

Andy Taylor's girlfriend had a funny last name. Other than that, she was more-or-less perfect: stunningly beautiful, no female neuroses about body image used as a method of birth control, and highly intelligent without being pretentious. She was funny and sexy and didn't just talk about herself all the time. She was impressed by the fact that Andy didn't need a gun to do the same job that other men needed a gun for. Helen Crump had it all.

She didn't drink too much or eat too little or take laxatives or smoke meth or cut her arms with a razor blade or fuck your best friend after the Lady Gaga concert. She was a schoolteacher and that was cool and her eyes, oh those eyes – green and penetrating and translucent like jade flickering under candlelight. Helen Crump may have had the most hypnotic eyes in the history of Hollywood except for Newman and Sinatra and theirs were blue and they were guys so Helen Crump was really in a class by herself.

Come to think of it, Andy didn't have much of a chance. Anyone would have been rendered defenseless by the charms and spell cast by Miss Helen Crump. She cooked and cleaned and dressed tastefully yet always with that hint of potential nymphomania. It was no surprise Andy married her. Wouldn't you? She had that "Cover-me-I'm-go-in' attitude. Did I mention that in terms of sex she believed in maintaining control but not too much control and that she was wise, reasonable, and self-sufficient? She was articulate, had a healthy relationship with her mother, and liked to try new things like bowling. She was strong when she wanted to be, which was most of the time, but she could also be soft and feminine and vulnerable like a girl. She could both bait a hook and clean a rainbow trout without making strange sounds about how gross it was, and she could whip up a meal out of almost anything.

In Mayberry, 1968, they were drinking sunshine, not moonshine, and some rooms of the house were still private, like the bedroom. Andy Taylor was so in love with Miss Helen Crump that when they got married they forgot to change her last name to Taylor, which was just fine thank you very much because what was in a name anyway? But by Matlock, thirteen years later, Helen's act had gotten old and she had cut her hair and started demanding a lot and complaining a lot and Andy became morbidly obese from eating Ritz crackers box after box and he came down with some serious heart trouble. But hey, after all those years, that shit happens.

On The House

Christmas morning, a white Christmas at that, and Arnold is in fine spirits. It has been two years to the day since his last drink, and he has learned all the AA clichés like *one day at a time, progress not perfection*, and *let go, let God*. He has been living under the pink cloud of sobriety and doesn't hate himself anymore. Even his wife, Carlotta, who nearly divorced him twice, seems to like him again.

The gifts are under the tree. Ornaments gleam and blinkers wink on and off. Carlotta is in the kitchen, her black hair tied up in a bun, baking a ham with slices of pineapple toothpicked to the top. She is getting ready for the relatives and the big Christmas dinner. Meanwhile, Arnold is in the living room watching TV, specifically the Mormon Tabernacle Choir singing festive yuletide offerings most angelically and magnificently arranged and with all the expected seasonal panache. A commercial comes on; Arnold channel surfs. Oprah features an impoverished village near Nairobi. The little black children wear broad smiles despite their plight, despite the fact they have almost no food, no water, no medicine. Essentially, they have nothing but each other. Every day they go to the river and fill plastic jugs with brown water, the same water in which they bathe, in which the animals defecate, and to make matters worse, several of the children are quarantined due to eating virus-riddled monkey meat. They have bumps and open sores from head to toe. Twenty per cent of the children born in this village will die before age five. Dysentery, malnutrition, and starvation are rampant.

Incredibly, in twenty-three minutes of Oprah, Arnold's pink cloud has darkened into a vicious shit storm and Arnold hates himself and Carlotta and God and all the American hedonism and narcissism and the excess tossed into the garbage from five-star restaurants which could easily feed these villagers like kings. He hates rock stars and movie stars and corporate thieves in three-piece suits who dupe ignorant politicians out of $700 billion (that's billion with a "b".) More than anything, he hates fucking Oprah who keeps saying that each of these villages could dig a well for just $5000, yet Oprah's worth $1.5 billion (that's billion with a "b"). Why doesn't she dig the goddamn wells? Why doesn't she save the destitute villagers? Two years sober, yet suddenly there is nothing in the world Arnold wants to do more than belt down a fifth of Bacardi, with the possible exception of sticking a ten millimeter Glock in his mouth and providing some new Christmas decor for the old wallpaper.

"What the hell is this?" Carlotta shrieks. She has opened one of Arnold's gifts. "I told you I wanted a sewing machine." It is more of a gag gift than anything, a pair of edible panties called "Choc-o-Thong." Arnold could imagine her later that night with a large bowl of French vanilla ice cream, crumbling the sexy confection all over the top like chocolate sprinkles. Arnold had read that women reached their sexual peak at age 40. Carlotta turned 40 in June, yet she and Arnold didn't even sleep in the same room.

Arnold knows if he watches another minute of Oprah he is going to spontaneously combust, or worse, and he wants to go buy something because that's what Americans do when they're desperate—buy shit they can't afford and don't need—the foundation of American gluttony. Unfortunately, all the department stores are closed. But fortunately, all the cocktail lounges are not, and that's what drunks do when they try to dodge disquieting emotions – get drunk. So he pulls on his boots and hat and coat and Carlotta barks, "Where in the hell are you going? They'll be here any minute!"

Arnold slams the front door and climbs in the car. He knows he has another relapse in him, but he is not sure he has another recovery. He should find an AA meeting but decides instead to check out The Silver Tap Bar and Grill to see if any of the old gang are celebrating the holidays. The descending snowflakes are immense, like millions of infant hands floating towards Earth. As the car slides around in the slush and ice and snow, he feels his spirit continue to tailspin in a downward spiral like a WWII fighter plane with a trail of black smoke in its wake. He should call his sponsor. He should call one of eleven phone numbers he has in his wallet. Instead, he keeps driving. A block from the tavern, he is waiting at a red light when he hears a scream. "HELP!"

He rolls down the window. A man has climbed a ladder and is standing on his pitched gable roof. He is holding a blow torch and was melting the snow and ice but has gone too far and now the house s on fire. As he tries to scurry down the ladder, he is shaking demonstrably and hyperventilating and the ladder has subsequently fallen in the snow-covered bushes below. "PLEASE, SOMEBODY, HELP!"

In a brief moment of clarity, Arnold realizes that he can't do anything for the children in Africa right now but he can try to save this crazy son of a bitch, so he throws the car in park, runs up to the house, and hoists the ladder up against the smoldering two-story duplex. He calls 9-1-1 on his cell and within minutes, the roar of the fire engine is audible in the distance. When the commotion dies down, the man with the blow torch offers Arnold a drink. Arnold smiles a little but declines, and the man thanks him profusely over and over again and hugs Arnold with tears in his eyes that are about to freeze. A news crew pulls up in a van, and a thin woman with blonde hair and a camel-hair coat asks Arnold how it feels to be a hero.

And later that night in bed with Carlotta, they watch the eleven o'clock news. "There is no such thing as a hero," Arnold says. "There are only average people like me trying to survive. And when it's over Carlotta whispers, "You're a hero to me, Snookie. You'll always be my hero." And she gets naked and steps into the chocolate thong, and Arnold gets busy and doesn't worry much about the calories because hey, after all, at least for another twenty-three minutes, it's still Christmas.

The Vinyl Shower Curtain Association

"As many as 100 toxic chemicals associated with adverse health effects are released in the air from polyvinyl chloride shower curtains. These chemicals make up that 'new shower curtain smell' unique to vinyl shower curtains and curtain liners. Though ubiquitous around the world, toxic chemical off-gassing may contribute to respiratory irritation, damage to the central nervous system, liver and kidney, nausea, headaches, loss of coordination, and contaminate the air we breathe." —Environmental News Network

It's three o'clock in the morning. Catastrophes always seem happiest at three o'clock in the morning. A high-ranking member of The Vinyl Shower Curtain Association calls an even higher-ranking member. Though it is a private line and routinely monitored for eavesdropping devices, the men speak in hushed code.

"The cattle are dying in the field."

"The turtle is boosting his shell.

In civilian terms, this means the news is out. PVC – polyvinyl chloride – is killing the universe one bathroom at a time. Difficult decisions must be made. Personal sacrifices are inevitable. Fortunes hang in the balance like house flies in a spider's architecture. Heavy fiscal casualties and vast collateral damage are likely. Extreme action, something demonstrable, has to be exacted immediately. But what damage control can be executed to stem the tsunami of this gathering disaster? PR spin doctors? Oil executives? For a calamity of this magnitude, only one rank of patriot is cunning enough—tobacco lobbyists! Tobacco lobbyists are hard-wired for insomnia and three a.m. calamaties. They aren't the last resort, they're the only resort.

"The fox is in the forest."

Within hours, The Vinyl Shower Curtain Association issues a press release replete with seamlessly plausible deniablilty. Along with the team from Philip Morris, Ivy League experts in tailor-made suits are summoned to debunk the liberal environmental agenda as they bathe in the artificial heat wave of 5000-watt spotlights. After the return volley, a significant salvo to say the least, there is nothing to do but wait. Wait and watch the quarterly profit margins. Wait and prepare to allay the fears of stockholders obsessed with short-term gains.

Afterwards, the members of The Vinyl Shower Curtain Association will bask in the refuge of their own private lavatories, and they will proceed to take very long, very hot showers because no matter what else may be said of them, they are not hypocrites. After all, they too are Americans, just like you and me. With families and cars and bills to pay. With the stars and stripes flying from a flagpole on their new redwood sundeck.

Tough Shit

> *Fossilized excrement found in an Oregon cave has given scientists the clearest evidence to date that humans roamed the world at least 1,000 years earlier than previously believed. The prehistoric feces, deposited in a cave some 14,300 years ago, contains DNA from the forebears of modern day Native Americans, according to the research.* —The Boston Globe

Og is not good with spears. He can sharpen them to a point, sneak up with great stealth on his prey, but he has poor aim. Too high or too low. Once he winged a bison and it nearly trampled him to death. Og's wife gives him the silent treatment. She has no more grunts or groans for him. Not even a dirty look. She does not care much for crude pictographs of wolves and goats etched on the stone walls of their cave in the Paisley neighborhood. Og's family hasn't eaten meat in eight days. His wife is gaunt. Og Jr. is wailing until the stone in the cave itself is bereft.

One morning, Og wakes well before dawn, dons his hides and wolf skins, and after a breakfast of roots and leaves sets out with his best new spear. Just after sunrise with the pink horizon beckoning the sky, he glimpses a camel near a stand of tall pines. Og is angry—angry at his wife, his son, his fate, the gods... He expects nothing but hurls the spear with all his pain and frustration in what would normally be a tragic trajectory but to his surprise and delight, it pierces the camel's heart straight on. The beast crumples and folds to the ground. Og runs to it frantically, fantastically, and embraces the dead dromedary. His own heart beats with a fevered percussion as he smears the camel's warm blood all over his face in celebration. He is a hunter. A hunter after all. He digs the organs from the camel's chest with a spearhead and returns to the cave in victory. Glorious. Triumphant. His wife eats ravenously and his young son. Their eyes are wild. Their faces contort into something like smiles as they feast. And when their bellies are full, Og will return to the carcass to harvest more of the kill but first, he stops at the final cave in the Paisley neighborhood, the cave at the edge of the forest, the prehistoric public toilet, the communal lavatory. He squats and defecates, relieving himself of a well-earned and satisfying bowel movement, one that will be remembered centuries after he is forgotten.

Equilibrium

During the war, Donald was the only fighter pilot on record with vertigo, an occupational hazard to be sure. Once he was shot down in a P38 Lockheed Lightning and crashed into the Pacific. Among the flotsam and jetsam of a Japanese destroyer, he found corpses and partial corpses floating and bobbing in the waves. For years after the war, he had a dream that severed arms were trying to grab him and drag him underwater. Even though he became a master gardener and an expert in flora and fauna, even though he had his own company and a wife he loved, he could not shake this dream. After awhile, he got used to it.

Shortly after he retired, his wife died of cancer. He joined the VFW hall on Sycamore Street. He was one of the older vets and sometimes they talked about the war—Eisenhower, Hitler, D-Day—but only in a vague sort of way. No one had the heart to discuss the battles, what they had seen, the nightmares they still dreamed. The first day of his membership, Donald was playing 8-ball with Maurice, a black man in the Navy during Nam. Maurice was a poor pool player but extremely comical. A real crack-up. One day Donald was lining up a four-ball in the side pocket when he noticed a painting of Napoleon on the wall. Napoleon was sitting on a horse and looking quite dignified but the painting was off-kilter, slightly askew, and Donald straightened it out. Maurice told him that his need to straighten the picture was something called "cognitive dissonance." It was the mind's need to make things right, to fix what was wrong, to put things in their proper place. In addition to being a comedian, Maurice was pretty smart, too.

Maybe because his wife had died or maybe because he sold his company, Donald spent more and more time at the VFW. But instead of drinking a few beers with the boys, he found himself drinking whiskey straight. A lot of whiskey straight. But what wasn't straight was that picture of Napoleon. It was never straight. No matter how many times he fixed it, it was always askew the next time he walked in the door. After awhile, that's the first thing he looked at when he entered the VFW. The Napoleon painting, constantly crooked and cock-eyed. Donald asked the owner about it, but all the owner could do was shrug. He had more important things on his mind. He had to order more whiskey.

Eventually, Donald just accepted the fact that Napoleon would always be tilted at a slight angle. He accepted the fact that he was drinking a lot, a bottle every day, and that his dream of drowning in the unfriendly waters of the Pacific Ocean would never go away. Even after he was pulled over by the cops one night for driving under the influence and thrown in jail, he just accepted the fact that that's the way things were. He and Napoleon, tilted, not quite right. And when Donald died of liver failure and a heart that had failed to straighten itself out, the only person at his funeral was Maurice with the picture of Napoleon under his arm and at an angle.

Technology Haiku

Smart car dead in ditch.
Assistance not forthcoming.
Camera phones shoot.

Linda's Home Improvement Loan

Linda went to the bank
borrowed $2,000

and gave it all
to her unemployed

uninspired boyfriend
Darnell. "Here," she said.

"Get out of my house."

Poetic Justice

occurred the day
the man
who designed
high heeled shoes
married
the woman
who invented
the necktie

Madalyn Murray O'Hair Faces God on Judgment Day

Oh shit.

Really?

It's Just Another Day

in Hell. *Breakin' Up Is Hard To Do*
by Neil Sedaka plays on an eternal loop.
Lucifer is lethargic as usual.
Idle hands aren't the devil's workshop.
Satan hasn't picked up a hammer in twelve thousand years.
The only souls toiling away now are serial killers,
crooked politicians & tow truck drivers
making the same metal ashtray into infinity.
Everyone thinks it's a blast furnace down here,
but it's so drafty we have to wear sweater vests.
What's more, hell isn't down at all.
Hang a left at heaven, go west about a light year,
you can't miss it.

Contrary to popular opinion,
money is not the root of all evil.
The devil can't even afford electricity.
Everyone walks around with flashlights
& those ridiculous miners' helmets
like they're digging for diamonds.
What really surprises me is no sex,
even though there's enough rock stars to fill a galaxy.
Motley Crue? Some of the nicest people I've ever met.
Ozzy Osbourne? Doesn't leave his lair except to pee.

Satan hates red.
He has no use for human sacrifice.
He's exhausted by the mere mention
of temptation or demonic possession.
Witches & heretics give him the silent treatment.
Rumor has it he tried to exorcise himself.

As for horns or a pointy tail—forget it.
He's clean shaven, 5'2", wears horn-rimmed glasses
& looks like Wally Cox.
I heard he even contacted the Almighty
for a game of seven-card-stud.
Hell sure ain't what it used to be.
It ain't even what it never was.
Of course, there's always a snowball's chance
the old boy will make a comeback,
& creep into your kitchen for a devil's food cupcake
in the middle of the night.

Tiger Tamer

Sara whispers into the soft ear hairs
of seven Bengal tigers
purring like kittens in a ton-and-a-half heap of fur.
They love the way she uses her whip
& especially the way she does not.

In another life they might be wandering dry stream beds
chasing down an antelope, crumpling a water buffalo
or hiding from poachers intent on grinding their balls
into the dust of an ancient aphrodisiac.
But in this life they live for Sara,

five-foot, ten-inch blonde & beautiful Sara,
who leaves their balls intact
& they don't mind standing on a chair for her
or dancing a little jig
or even playing dead.

Don't Read This Poem

unless your glass is half-full
unless you're willing to believe
that for every pissed-off tornado
like the one in *The Wizard of Oz*
there is a sweet sister-twister
like the whirlwind in St. Mary's, Kansas, 1993.

Ma asleep for hours,
I hit the rack around midnight.
Pa stumbles home drunk as usual
fumbles to find his key
but there is no keyhole
because there is no house.
The old, white A-frame is now perched a hundred feet away

with uncanny symmetry on top of the barn.
as Ma & I snooze dreamily inside
heirloom china neither chipped nor cracked
antique crystal in mint condition
no farm girls struck on the head
no animals killed or unaccounted for
just a friendly pick-me-up from a lonely cyclone
roaming through Tornado Alley on a Saturday night
with God's fingerprint swirls all over it.

Four miles down the road
the torrent spins a glorious pit stop
through O'Malley's greenhouse
plucks a sizable garden of pink gardenias
& twirls its way through the state of Kansas
a resplendent vacuum of positive energy
a tap-dancing pink tornado of love.

Poetry Graveyard

This is the bottom
of my bottom desk drawer
where the corpses of verse mix & frolic
in the middle of the night
when all else is silent save the howl of the dog
from the door of a distant hen house.

These are the lost poems from a decade of students
who missed the last class, bailed out on the workshop
relocated to Kansas City or somewhere near Kansas City
disconnected phone number, no forwarding address
the students who went to lunch & never came back.
It happens that way sometimes, they simply disappear.

Is it a crisis of faith?
Has the language committed infidelity?
Maybe they're not ready
to stand in the rain like a lightning rod.
Maybe the altitude
has worked its card trick vertigo.

I am the repository
for a circus of souls, angels, clinging hearts
an extended metaphor of chocolate & sex
pain worn on the lapel like a price tag
clichés tossed together at random
on the discount clearance rack.

I've learned to sleep sitting up
with one eye open
& a red pen in hand
because they're all in the bottom
of my bottom desk drawer
plotting & scheming to revise.

Endangered Species

before John James Audubon learned to fence or dance
before he learned to ride horses or play violin
& long before he cultivated his obsession
to paint every bird in North America
he had a conversation with his heart

one night he sat across the table from it
not a dream of it, not the idea of it
but an actual human heart—his heart
which had escaped from his chest & sat facing him

even as it leaked red on the dining room carpet
even as the arteries & capillaries wriggled into position
to catch every scrap of the ensuing debate
young J.J. knew it was a discussion to be embraced, not feared

yes, he said, *I know you will pump blood*
to every hamlet in the geography of my body
yes, I know you will suffer heartache, heartbreak, even heart attack
with every girl who looks your way & smiles with her eyes

& yes I know absence will make you grow fonder
all the while the heart perched itself, removed & indifferent
smug, unable to be reasoned with
but soon that heart would climb back inside the chest

of John James Audubon & beat like the wings
(of) a calliope hummingbird native to North America
metallic green back & crown white gorget with purple rays,
courting the female
trying to protect the species from extinction
from the pain of losing the last lover on Earth
that could ever really love him back

Alchemy

azure eyes scan hundreds of sailors
dazzling as human snow drifts in their Navy whites
when she laser locks on her man
her husband, the father of her children
she no longer needs her sense of sight

"Darrell," she screams
from now on, she no longer needs a sense of sound
she's had 18 months of wartime silence
the rare, abbreviated phone call from the war zone
riddled with static
sounds from concerned teachers, bill collectors
her mother, her sister, her boss

when she reaches him, embraces him
it is everything she dreamed of
she can defy gravity without gravity's consent
347 nights of remembering their engagement, wedding, babies
she holds him so close the blood rushes to his head
so close the seagulls hover to see if he will break
she smells him – not cologne or a special soap but him, just him
& no longer needs her sense of smell

as she sobs into his shoulder
as they share the most private moment of their lives
she feels his musculature, his beard, his heartbeat
& when she can tear her arms from around him
they will share a long, slow movie star kiss
a kiss to end all kisses
which will redefine her sense of touch

this morning, a Saturday at the Bremerton Naval Station
there is something in the air like love, but better
there is something in the air so powerful
that calling it love isn't enough
because love is also the score of zero in tennis
someone loves a good movie or a new pair of shoes
this is something more than love
this is what keeps the rest of us vicariously alive

Ken's Lament

Mattel vice-president of marketing Russell Arons announces Barbie and Ken will part ways after 43 years together, February 12, 2004

Whatever happened to Ballroom-Barbie
the pink taffeta gown with spaghetti straps?
Or Tennis-Barbie in those blinding tennis whites?
Or Barbie-at-the-Beach in the neon yellow one-piece?

Now it's Wheelchair-Barbie and Chinese-Barbie
and caramel-skinned African-American-Barbie
(a.k.a. "Sheneequah-LaFaunna-Barbie")
and Jewish-Barbie and Muslim-Behind-A-Veil-Barbie
and every politically correct Barbie imaginable
in this United Nations of Barbies.
Goth-Barbie, Satanic High-Priestess Barbie,
Angry-Radical-Feminist-Venom-Dripping-Off –The-Fangs-
Barbie and whose idea
was Demolition-Expert-Barbie with real blasting caps?
Where will this kaleidoscope end?
How about Corporate-Bitch-In-A-Three-Piece-Suit-
Who-Won't-Return-My-Phone-Calls-Barbie?

What happened to us, baby?
If you're bored with my look I could exchange the sweater
for black leather chaps or get a body part pierced.
I could tattoo your name on my plastic bicep.
But there's not much time.
They're about to phase me out like the Pet Rock.
This is an SOS for the only Barbie who can save me now:
Special-Ops-Barbie with night vision goggles
desert camouflage fatigues,
and a shoulder-harnessed surface-to-air missile.
(batteries not included).

Ken's Reconciliation

Valentine's Day, 2006

if I could only hold you
in my non-malleable arms
or kiss you the way they do on TV
where I met you in that 1961 commercial
plastic love at first sight

but this is not the time to complain
for my Barbie has come back to me
& there is no need to explain about Blaine
the boogie boarder from The Land Down Under
I will love you in perpetuity, my darling

even when the feminists & sociologists
call you "…an evil incantation of the female form
to an unattainable male…"
I will always love you Barbie Millicent Roberts

since you went away I have dated every doll in Toys R Us
questioned my own sexuality with GI Joe
& one night even found myself

in an adult movie theater
removing body parts from Mr. Potato Head
but now you're back, my precious love
& we'll never be apart again
no matter what
no matter how much money it makes
for the pimps of corporate America

Tennis Racket

—for Uncle John

Today is June 6, 1994, "D-Day Plus Fifty."
The country I live in commemorates
this the lynchpin of the 20th century
with a fine parade, speeches, a barbeque.
Fifty years ago
just hours before the largest military operation in history
someone said, "Everything is at stake."

An old G.I. on TV recalls
the blood-red waters at Omaha Beach
mortars & machine gun fire
dead corpses floating everywhere
limbs, torsos, smoke & fire.

He crawls up the beach
some time after the first wave
to the foot of the cliffs
to the stacks of gear, weapons & ammo
to the boots, clothes, helmets
& rows of dead soldiers.

A tear wells up in his eye
as he relates how he found a tennis racket, of all things
lying there in perfect condition
& how peculiar it was to find
a tennis racket
amidst the chaos & terror on that beach.
"Leave it to an American, " he half-laughs, half cries.

The TV special ends & I go to bed thinking about the old soldier
what it must've been like:
the explosions, blood in the sand
the smell of death.
I wonder if years later
when he returned home from the war
if he ever picked up a tennis racket
leisurely hit a few balls over the net. Just for fun.

Another Pop Icon Obsession

Britney Spears' navel shadows me
like the piercing eye of a Sacred Heart painting.
Though I attempt to wiggle & writhe away
her navel stalks me, grows legs & walks be-
hind me, through skyscraper silhouettes late at light
the worst neighborhood in town.
Finally I collapse from fear & exhaustion.

Daybreak, an urban cemetery,
Britney Spears' navel on a rooftop across the street
flirts with sharpshooters as I unwittingly pose for one clean shot.
I run again & she chases me, gains on me
through the swish of Midwestern cornfields
to the heights of the open air stream
'til I'm breathless, delirious, & fall to Earth
in the middle of a farmer's field
smack dab in the center of perfectly concentric crop circles
& somewhere inside this soybean geometry
a black hole
swirls.

I know what I have to do—
climb inside & crawl through this darkness into a new world
free of infatuation & obsession
a place on the ocean floor where bioluminescent creatures
brighten the depths like negligees with neon eyes
lingerie fluttering on a clothesline.
This is where creatures live in the dark
able to create their own light,
winking & blinking
sometimes to attract a mate,
sometimes to hunt prey,
but always flashing signs of love & death in random order.

Stopping For Directions

place your right hand on the green spot
feel the process of chlorophyll
as your right hand becomes green
as your arms, torso, legs, hair become green
instruct your partner to place left foot on blue
soon your partner will be as blue as the sea
& sky colliding
this is your cue to make love
to create one red child & one yellow child
to fill your world with primary colors
it is undeniably beautiful now
but you know, somehow
it will never be enough

try this:
discard map, compass, scalpel
organize an expedition into your personal archeology
search for the lost era known as fourth grade
touch the stalagmites, enjoy the familiar smell
you missed this detour a while back, my friend

now is the time to ride a horse
get your picture in the paper
learn French
call the one person you'd call
if you had an hour left to live

you have just enough time
to build a fort in the woods
identical to the one in fourth grade

you built with your friends after school
with the rope ladder & corrugated roof
no deviations, no alterations, no ornamentations

see how you've corrected your trajectory?
the hemispheres of your brain are engaged in a tango
a torrid love affair of fruit & fire
synergy surges through your bloodstream
flowing all the way to your fingertips
requiring the thermoregulation of every color in your chemistry
& silence the sole method of birth control

Directions to my island girlfriend

there's no street address
look for the large hut
behind the clump of palms
next to the white beach
where Chamorro kids
drink cheap beer all night
& listen to hiphop
down the dirt road from the big market
(the fish market,
not the farmer's market)
then make a sharp right
ask around—you'll find it
if you've gone to the volcano
or sacred ancestral burial grounds
you've gone too far

Twenty Years Ago

I remember back in the old college days
when you were raped on a Friday night in Tucson
a cowboy filled with painkillers & tequila
knocked on your apartment door
begging to use the phone
then he raped you
then he raped you again
then he fell asleep in your bed
so you called the cops
& the next morning's headline read: *Zzzzzzzz*
I was going to write a letter to the editor, but I didn't

a few weeks later, the Todd Rundgren concert
you had to drive my car
because the hit of acid I did with dinner
left trails of taillights
red blurs smeared down the highway
& after the concert you drove to the airport
became a silver jet, vanished into a cloud
& how you ever survived I'll never know
but I'm still waiting for you here at Gate C

Unsolicited Material

May I speak to Mike Hickey, please.

    This is he.

Hi. This is Connie from Good Samaritan Hospital.
You were in last week for a physical examination. Correct, sir?

    That's right.

Dr. Morris asked you to send a stool sample.
Have you had a chance to do that yet?

    Yes, I did.

Are you sure?

    Believe me, Connie. I would remember
    fishing a turd out of the toilet with a plastic bag.
    I mailed it in a large manila envelope.

That night under the coffee table
I find a large manila envelope
addressed to Good Samaritan Hospital
containing a self-addressed stamped envelope
a short biography & five perfectly typed
laser-printed poems, white as starched collars,
and a brief cover letter:

    Attention: Poetry Editor / *The New Yorker*
    I have enclosed the following for your consideration…

Several months later I return from work one day
to find a large manila envelope wedged in the mailbox
containing my bag of petrified shit.

"We regret that we are unable
to use the enclosed material.
Thank you for giving us the
opportunity to consider it."—THE EDITORS

Direction of the Spiral

for Martha Clarkson

1.

Late sunlight dashes like a jailbreak
through a canopy of conifer trees,
rests on Sheila, cross-legged in a bed of needles.
Her fingers twist spirals of hair
the color of pennies flattened on a railroad track.
She ruminates & chain smokes:
"Wait until your father gets home
from work, young lady.
All hell's gonna break loose."

I hate being seventeen. I hate my parents.
I wish I was dead.
She considers igniting a forest fire.
How could I leave my diary unlocked?

Billy Palmer had my bra unhooked
before I could resist another kiss.
I like sex. Planned Parenthood.
Birth control pills.
Connie Sullivan's pot party.
I stole the purse from Woolworth's
just to see if I could.
Stupid. Stupid. Stupid.

"You can forget New York, Missy.
No acting classes, no Broadway,
no *New York Times* reviews or Tony Awards,"

her mother, the snoop, lashes out.
"You'll be lucky to go to junior college."
Sheila's greatest fear in life: being ordinary.

2.

Eventually Sheila returns to the forest.
Night drops its dark veil
around the orange glow of her cigarette.
Mother was right, there were no awards
no neon lights on Broadway
just a junior college in Davenport, Iowa
teaching eighteen years' worth of drama classes
voice projection & method acting.
Become the character.
Sheila recalls a student named Paul
a distant boy with freshly divorced parents.
His mother threw him out of the house
when she found his porno mags.

After class one day he blushes.
His soft eyes confide, confess, that acting class saved him.
For the first time in his life
he can feel himself breathe again.
For the first time in his life
the blood in his veins pulse like an armada on attack.
He feels like he can accomplish anything.
Everything.
And at that moment,
Sheila is extraordinary.

The House Across the Street

In nine years: never had a barbeque with them, never traded stories over the fence, never said hello, not even once. So when the couple across the street moves out, I vow to woo the new neighbors and create a sense of community. The monolithic yellow moving van rolls up on a Monday morning in July. I'm late to work but promise myself that later, I'll bake them a Bundt cake or maybe offer to mow the lawn.

A short round woman, a small blonde daughter, & a white cat with a collar that jingles—I see all three sitting on the porch one warm night with the trellis & clapboard, something icy to drink, beads of condensation slide down the side of the glass in a Tennessee Williams motif. I want to offer salutations from under the street lamp:

hey neighbor!
still in boxes?
I live over here…
my name is . . .
if you need anything . . .

But I don't.

This morning I am smoking a cigarette on the front stoop. The new neighbors' white cat sashays along the sidewalk on my side of the street, jingles the collar bell & eyeballs me suspiciously as the wind snatches a handful of my smoke. This makes the feline nervous & unsettled & as a car approaches, the cat makes a fantastic last dash at the worst possible moment.

The car drives on, the cat trembles, a final frantic dinging of the bell then stops twitching. I carry the animal limp in my arms across the street, Aloha Avenue. The round woman cries, her daughter says, *look, kitty's eyes are still open—she's alive*!

I close the cat's eyes, wrap it in an old beach towel & bury it in their backyard with a square-head shovel. This is my house-warming present, my special welcome-to-the-neighborhood gift. The girl pulls a nasturtium from the garden, plants it in the moist earth of the fresh grave. She & her mother thank me, hug me, in the way strangers embrace strangers & survivors hold survivors when they share something too painful for words. And I leave without asking their names, without really wanting to know.

The House I Grew Up In

Weeds wage
a hostile takeover
of the lawn.
Tendrils of dandelions
tether together
drift & float
through their ballet
of insurrection. The hedges,
now more than hedges,
are determined
to swallow the house whole.
Foundation cracked,
maple trees dead,
roof peeling layers of skin.
Father emerges through the threshold.
Since mother died in '78
& the kids slipped away
with their dreams & bandages
under the cover of darkness,
he has surrendered to the elements
& walks the sidewalk to greet me,
his hair a white flag.
Suddenly, three trespassers on bikes
tear across the yard.
One glances at my father.
I didn't know anybody lived here,
he says & the three of them
fly down the driveway
escape through the backyard
to destinations unknown

territories uncharted.
Come inside, son,
my father says.
Make yourself at home.

My Life as a Woman from Cleveland

I tell my shrink I sometimes feel
like I'm living the life of another person.

So who are you, he asks,
a woman from Cleveland?

Yes, a tall woman with auburn hair, hazel eyes.
In my day I had hips that could topple a man like a wheat thrasher.

I have four kids but they don't call me anymore.
My husband died long ago, I don't remember how.

My dog is a golden retriever named Ginger.
She enjoys digging up the yard,

which is okay by me.
Sometimes I like to dig a hole or two myself.

A couple years ago
I drank a bottle of malt liquor by ten a.m. every day.

Then I took up religion, yoga, the saxophone,
tap dancing, clipped coupons, collected coins,

saved box tops, joined a canasta tournament
& met a man named Frank who serviced vending machines

but he only wanted a piece of ass.
So I went back to walking Ginger downtown

sometimes to the library, Jacobs Field, the Rock 'n' Roll Museum
but now Ginger has died & I want to reinvent myself,

remix my x-rays from the inside out
transform into someone completely new & exciting

a poet perhaps, possibly a man from Seattle
someone whose life isn't nearly as bad as he thinks.

My Next-Door Neighbor Robyn

is seven years old.
Her father is a physicist
but she can't pronounce "physicist"
so she tells her friends at school
that her daddy sells shoes.
The day after
her father's funeral,
I teach her to say "phy-si-cist"
one syllable at a time,
but she doesn't understand
what the word means.
She prefers the word "gossamer."
It is her favorite word.

I Should Tell You Right Now

for my son Nathan

it looks more
like an alien archive shot
from Area 51
or a satellite photo
from a Level Three hurricane
but it is you, my son
alive in your mother's womb
heart beating like the frantic wings of a hummingbird
both real & surreal
I love you already
even though you're just the size of an avocado
you carry the weight of the moon in your hands
haikus in your eyes
& your impressive little penis
but I should tell you right now
I don't golf, play poker
or go to the race track
& the last time I went fishing
I accidentally poked the eye
out of a rainbow trout
as I tried to set him free

Mutter-in-Law

She moves in on a Thursday at your wife's behest and miraculously on Friday you find the carpet clean, the laundry folded, and dinner on the table. Just make sure you like squid: fried squid, grilled squid, squid paté, squid-on-a-stick.

And if you get tired of squid and decide to make a sandwich, you'll find the bread in the freezer because she's from a small island in the South Pacific where bread gets moldy at an accelerated rate and even if you buy a second loaf just for yourself, both will be in the freezer by the end of the week.

And it won't be long before your favorite piece of art, a reproduction of Picasso's "Blue Nude," is hidden behind the recycling bin in the garage because she doesn't want to see a naked woman's body on the living room wall while watching *Golden Girls*.

And despite what anyone says, orchids are easy to grow, Barbara Bush was a hula hoop champion, the pope drinks champagne not wine, and there is a species of spider that has only seven legs and sings like a mockingbird when the moon is full.

And she likes to spritz Chanel #5 on the baby's head even though she knows it gives him a rash.

And I know you'll understand when you find the Persian rug rolled up and stashed next to Picasso despite the fact that it was in the living room specifically to prevent nicks in the new bamboo floor from your four-year-old's toy trucks. And why has she removed this rug? Come on, you know. Because it reminds her of a carpet from her mother-in-law.

The Embalmer's Son

Roger vows that when he dies
he will not succumb to the whims of his father,
the sinister minister, Roger Sr.
Booneville County's embalmer extraordinaire,
the man with all the answers for this life, the next life,
and for 24 easy payments, the life in-between.

Roger resolves not to be dipped in a vat of daddy's formaldehyde
blood drained & lips pinned closed,
the begrudging smile of a suicide's mouth.
Roger will not be arranged in a velvet box like a strand of pearls,
propped up by titanium supports,
battery-powered quadraphonic sound
& an old baseball mitt
arranged to make him appear natural, content.

No, when the creation of Roger is over,
the cremation of Roger begins,
his ashes spread inconspicuously
to the handful of airports around the country
that still have ashtrays.
Roger wants to fly under the radar
no headlights, spotlights, searchlights,
out from under the heavy scrutiny,
of ex-bosses, ex-wives, ex-friends.

Roger just wants to fit in.
Roger just wants to be left alone.
Roger wants to remain anonymous except, perhaps,
to that proud contingent of maintenance personnel
cleaning our nation's airports who would instantly recognize
these are not just any ashes.
These are the ashes of Roger.

The Suicide Squeeze

in terms of physics
there is a slight
almost imperceptible
advantage to sliding
into home plate
head first vs. legs first

it takes approximately
.003 of a second
to swing your hips

still, you are less likely
to get injured
if you slide legs first
than head first
because feet and ankles
are less breakable
than fingers and hands

so which is best
head first
or legs first?
the truth is
you're probably
going to be best
at whichever way
you feel
most comfortable
just be sure
you decide in advance
so you don't try

to do both
simultaneously
& corkscrew yourself
into the dirt
it's your choice
but it never hurts to do
a little risk assessment
from time to time
does it?

The Evolution of Anger

After church, George wanders through the store
in search of dinner as he ponders the preacher's sermon
about a third century Christian who said,
Be kind, for everyone you meet is fighting a great battle.

George browses through Frozen Foods
Nancy Sinatra doing "These Boots Are Made For Walkin'"
& three shoppers in three different aisles harmonize,
One of these days these boots are gonna walk all over you.

George suspects not much has changed since the third century
as a young toddler screams for a lollipop in Aisle #3.
His mother ignores him as long as she can.
If you scream again, I swear I'll slap your face.

The little boy is quiet now.
George gets his dinner—a beef pot pie.
Tension is bubbling in the human era like a stew, he thinks.
The cashier asks *paper or plastic*?

George wonders if she's angry
so many people need consolation
so many people eat frozen food
whatever feels right to you, George says.

Part of the Jar Is Still Empty

I drink late in the afternoon
at a downtown tavern in Tucson.
Every thirsty patron who opens the door
unleashes a flashflood of desert sunlight
which blinds the crowd like a deity.

The bartender makes change
for an old-timer perched next to me
who drinks whiskey, sings off-key
and delicately turns over each quarter
(only quarters, not nickels or dimes).
He studies both sides of the coin
meticulously as an archeologist picking through fossils.
Why?

"I'm seventy-eight years old, son.
Outlived the wife, Mavis, by twelve years.
She got to saving things:
buttons, pine cones, and the like.
Took to collecting Bicentennial quarters
in a pickle jar on the nightstand.
I wish she would've told me those were fancy quarters.
One day I used them clean up for beer money.
She cried that night, died the next day.
I think I broke her heart to death.
So I keep searching for fancy quarters
to fill up that jar. Part of the jar is still empty—
that's where I live."

I give the old-timer all my quarters
and as he checks each side, I escape
to face the liquid desert sun.

Tuesday

in memory of my mother

you're on stage
in your underwear with the torn elastic waist
forgot to wear makeup
stage lights, cameras, close-ups
a billion viewers in 137 countries
you keep thinking it's a dream, but it's not
you wear a top hat, ride a unicycle, juggle flaming batons
crack the whip at the big cats
feel the heat of their breath
as they eye you like an appetizer
begin to spin fine china
thousands & thousands of plates on towering sticks
in the background there is wild music – *Sabre Dance*
playing at a fugitive tempo
karma & centrifugal force infiltrate the auditorium
distant constellations revolve around one another
you catch a glimpse of Ed Sullivan in the wings
tossing back a pitcher of martinis
you remember Jimmy needs a ride home from band practice
oh look, your boss is in the front row
he waves, he wants to have an affair with you
you cannot wave back because the plates
are losing momentum & when this grand finale concludes
on a Tuesday in February, 1978
there is a thunder & lightning reception for all
applause that registers as an earthquake
adulation that cracks foundations, sounds like a war
& it will carry you, this reward, for an eternity
to heights even the trapeze artists can't touch

The Comeback

People walk out and find
The trees discussing religion,
And how to hold your arms when it rains.
—William Stafford, "Forestry"

Sipping gin & tonic on a supersonic jet
This is the trip he has outmaneuvered
Like a pedestrian dodging traffic against the light
His mother was 48 when cancer reigned victorious
Now 48 himself, he should fear the disease
But is more afraid of the oak tree

He arrives at the cemetery
Steps out of the rental car, approaches the grave
Orchids & wisteria lie in repose
There, just behind the arboretum
just behind the marble headstone
In the midst of towering maples & sycamores
Stands the distilled oak

He was 21 when they last met
& recalls that day in October
Fists crashing into the trunk, over & over until
Uncle Ray wrapped arms around & subdued him
Those fists should have been broken in 17 places
But the next day remained unmarked

Now he pats the tree like an old friend
Examining the bark for bruises
Sorry, he says in a low tone, *I didn't mean it*
Songbirds are suddenly still
As the oak tree responds
I've been waiting for you

& drops a fluttering gold leaf in his direction
The man stares down at the grave
Speaks in whispers to the woman
Who gave him everything
Everything
Then kisses the grass
& flies away to the place he calls home
To the key under the welcome mat

Prepare for Take-off

April, 1995. I flew to Washington D.C. for my old university friend's wedding, but the entire weekend was a drag. I didn't know many people, and the ones I met were basically snobs. Plus, that asshole Timothy McVeigh had just blown up the federal building in Oklahoma City. It was all over the news, and no one was in a very festive mood. Plus, I'd been trying to stay balanced on the wagon and booze was everywhere, so I fell off hard. I did some sightseeing the day before the wedding, which was pretty cool for a history buff like me. It was a transcendent moment to stand at 1600 Pennsylvania Avenue and view the White House. It was breathtaking to see the Washington Monument and the Lincoln Memorial. But frankly, when the weekend ended, I was anxious to get back home to Seattle. Hung over and exhausted, I stepped aboard the airplane and into a major complication.

"I'm sorry, sir," the flight attendant in her crisp white shirt with gold embroidery said. "We're going to be delayed." She nodded toward a young boy across the aisle. "We're having a bit of a disciplinary issue with our friend Aaron over here."

A handful of nearby passengers silently corroborated her story with their sour looks.

Aaron had a shock full of blond hair with a cowlick, big green eyes, and that "Dennis the Menace" look of mischievousness, like, doesn't anyone know how to have fun around here? It seems that with his parents' blessing, Aaron had taken a plane all by himself from St. Louis to DC to visit his grandmother. Apparently he wasn't too keen on returning to mom and dad. I shot him a wink and smile. "I think Aaron and I are about to become good friends. Please sit us next to each other and, if possible, may we have two coloring books, some crayons, chocolate chip cookies, and a double vodka tonic—no lime."

The attendant smiled as if to say, sir, you have no idea how deep the shit pit is that you just stepped into. "Are you absolutely sure, sir? He's been kicking the backs of chairs and throwing tantrums left and right."

"I'm sure. Aaron and I are gonna be just fine."

"Thank you so much, sir," the flight attendant said. And she really meant it. I don't know what transpired before I stepped onto the aircraft, but that woman had more genuine concern and authenticity in her voice than anyone I've ever heard say anything in my entire life. "Your cocktails are complimentary." Then she smiled and whispered, "I prayed for a miracle and someone sent you."

Other passengers collectively smiled, nodded, and waved. They were pleased and relieved to have avoided further delay. But somehow, I sensed it was more than that. I had become their fearless leader of the open skies. I sensed they would be retelling this tale at the next barbeque or family reunion. I was their hero. Still, despite said heroism, I felt some trepidation. Two men across the aisle looked at me like, dude, what in the hell are you thinking?

"How old are you, Aaron?" I asked. He was a cute little boy, seven or eight years old I guessed, and a sparkle in his eye that suggested he was deep in thought. Maybe he was even reassessing his life. Maybe the entire world wasn't against him after all.

I really wanted to get off on the right foot with Aaron, and it seemed he shared the sentiment. With absolutely no forewarning, Aaron cocked his spring-loaded foot back and kicked me in the right shin. The blow was so vicious and the pain so volcanic that I screamed and pancaked onto the cabin floor. Little Aaron was like some crazed miniature field goal kicker winding up his leg with extra oomph because the wind was in his face. The fact is, to be truly accurate, Aaron didn't really kick my shin as much as kick *through* my shin. This is not uncommon for field goal kickers. Kick *through* the ball.

The pain marched resolutely in formation up my spinal cord and mushroomed. Finally it exploded into millions of charged pulsations and shocked 437,217 separate nerve endings, which had been positioned at every conceivable crossroads of my anatomy. It seemed clear that my new chum, Aaron, had just broken something, maybe a fibula. I don't know what a fibula is exactly, but I remember thinking it could be a fibula. Tears rolled down my cheeks. My leg throbbed intensely. It hurt more than the time I stepped on a five-inch nail at a construction site, more than the time I ran over my foot with a Toro lawnmower, and even more than the time I accidentally hit myself in the head with a sixteen-ounce framing hammer.

I'm not sure where I got the inspiration for my next line, but clearly there were powerful forces guiding my spirit. I stood six inches from Aaron's precious face and shouted, "I'll bust out that fucking window and throw your little ass 30,000 feet straight down if you do that again."

This got Aaron's attention and that of the other passengers as well. A gauntlet of faces up and down the plane gaped at me like I was a madman, which is quite silly, of course, because I'm not strong enough to bust out an airplane window – not that I hadn't imagined what that might look like. One by one, my fellow passengers began to smile and nod. I was battle-tested and combat-ready. They stowed their carry-ons and buckled their seatbelts. All was finally right in the world of United Airlines Flight 418 – DC to St. Louis.

Over the next three hours, Aaron and I became best friends. He colored and ate cookies. I colored and drank Smirnoff. Every time he finished a page, he showed it to me and I did the same. We talked about our favorite planets, why girls don't like to get dirty at recess, and if you were a dinosaur would you rather be a T-Rex or a pterodactyl? And it wasn't just that perfunctory airline banter, either. We talked about our families. We talked about why soccer was better than Cub Scouts. (Apparently there is no kicking in Cub Scouts.) And after Aaron and I got to know each other, to care about each other, I was sad to see the flight end. Of the six billion people on Planet Earth, two had managed to happily co-exist for three hours at the cost of a single injured appendage.

Despite his attempt to cripple me, Aaron proved to be quite bright and convivial. I was able to see his good side with a little prayer, a lot of patience, and several double vodka tonics. Aaron and I exchanged smiles. Our shared time on this planet was about to end.

When we touched down on the tarmac and rolled to a stop at the Lambert-St. Louis International Airport, every passenger on the plane – coach, first-class, even the three flight attendants—stood and clapped. Then the pilot and co-pilot emerged from the cockpit and applauded as well. It was like an after-school movie special and I was the star.

My proud co-star, Aaron, waved to the folks in back. People shook our hands as they disembarked and wished us good luck. As I limped off the aircraft, I paused to meet Aaron's parents. They were young, somewhere in their twenties, and extremely grateful. I bet they had some hellacious bruises themselves.

The airline officials asked if I wanted a free upgrade for my connecting flight to Seattle, but I declined. My reward was that I had earned Aaron's hard-earned respect. My reward was that I knew if it was a close call on Judgment Day, this might be enough to tip the scales in my favor.

February, 2012. Judgment Day has been on my mind since my dear old Uncle Jack died last month. In a final letter to the family he wrote:

Please do not be sad. If everything works out right, I'll be seeing my heavenly Father. If not, pray that I can meet with Him and maybe talk my way in...

Uncle Jack was eloquently loquacious. I'm not sure if I could talk my way in, but my day with Aaron might be my best shot. I was in a dark place, darker than I even realized, and perhaps my foray into Aaron's life was a form of atonement. I have a lot to atone for.

Nowadays I also have a son who is almost Aaron's age. Often I wonder if I'm sending my boy into a world of benevolent strangers or mad bombers like Timothy McVeigh.

Day by day, I understand a little bit more about why Aaron decided to kick me. His world needed kicking. Mine did, too. Perfect timing. He was doing us both a favor as he was doing his best to survive.

OTHER BOOKS BY MICHAEL G. HICKEY

PRAISE FOR *In Defense of Eve*

"*In Defense of Eve* is a delight—one lively, well-framed moment after another. I very much admire Hickey's wit and comic timing."

—Stephen Dunn, Pulitzer Prize for Poetry, 2001

"Michael G. Hickey? This poet is ALIVE! Celebrate his gusto, his wit and vivid voice—read his work!"

—Naomi Shihab Nye, recipient of four Pushcart prizes and the Paterson Poetry Prize

"Michael G. Hickey captures the mysterious quality of ordinary life in his chapbook, *In Defense of Eve*. His wry voice reinvents what he observes, from 7-Eleven's to Talk Shows to Tilt-A-Whirls, and makes us imagine our lives in new ways."

—Maura Stanton, Yale Series of Younger Poets Award, 1975

PRAISE FOR *Counterclockwise*

"One of the best pieces I've read all year. The opulence of Troy's glass ranch in the desert is reminiscent of Xanadu and *The Great Gatsby*. This is excellent work."

—Charles Johnson, 1990 National Book Award winner for *Middle Passage*